W9-CDI-201

LAUGH OUT LOUD!

THE CRAZY COMPUTERS JOKE BOOK

Sean Connolly and Joe Harris

WINDMILL BOOKS

New York

Published in 2013 by Windmill Books, An Imprint of Rosen Publishing
29 East 21st Street, New York, NY 10010

First Edition

Editor: Joe Harris
Illustrations: Adam Clay (cover) and Dynamo Design (interiors)
Layout Design: Notion Design

Library of Congress Cataloging-in-Publication Data

Connolly, Sean.
 The crazy computers joke book / by Sean Connolly and Joe Harris. — 1st ed.
    p. cm. — (Laugh out loud)
 Includes index.
 ISBN 978-1-61533-643-2 (library binding) — ISBN 978-1-61533-652-4 (pbk.) —
 ISBN 978-1-61533-653-1 (6-pack)
 1. Electronic data processing—Juvenile humor. 2. Computers—Juvenile humor. 3. Riddles, Juvenile. I. Harris,
Joe. II. Title.
 PN6231.E4C68 2013
 818'.602—dc23

                              2012019529

Printed in China

CPSIA Compliance Information: Batch #AW3102WM: For Further Information contact Windmill Books, New York, New York at 1-866-478-0556
SL002421US

CONTENTS

CRAZY COMPUTERS

Why did the robot leave school so young?
He was always being upgraded.

Teacher: Can you give me an example of software?
Pupil: A wool sweater?

Where is the world's biggest computer?
In New York—it's the Big Apple!

Who is a robot's favorite cartoon character?
Tin-tin!

Why did the medical computer go to prison?
It had performed an illegal operation.

CRAZY COMPUTERS

Where does the biggest spider in the universe live? On the World Wide Web.

What do you call a man with a speedometer in the middle of his forehead? Miles!

How do computers say goodbye? "See you later, calculator!"

Teacher: Steven, what's a computer byte? Pupil: I didn't even know they had teeth!

What do you get if you cross a computer with a lifeguard? A screensaver.

CRAZY COMPUTERS

Why are birds always on the Internet?
They just love tweeting.

What was the robot doing at the gym?
Pumping iron.

Why did the robot boxer sit on the stove before the big match?
He wanted to strike while the iron was hot.

Which cookie do computers like best?
Chocolate microchip.

If human babies are delivered by stork, how are robot babies delivered?
By crane!

CRAZY COMPUTERS

What did the computer nerd say when his mom opened the curtains?
Wow, look at those graphics!

Why are evil robots so shiny?
Because there's no rust for the wicked.

Did you hear about the kid who had his ID stolen?
Now he's just a "k."

Spotted in the library:
Robots Are People Too by Anne Droid.

What happened to the robot
who put his shoes on the wrong feet?
He had to be rebooted.

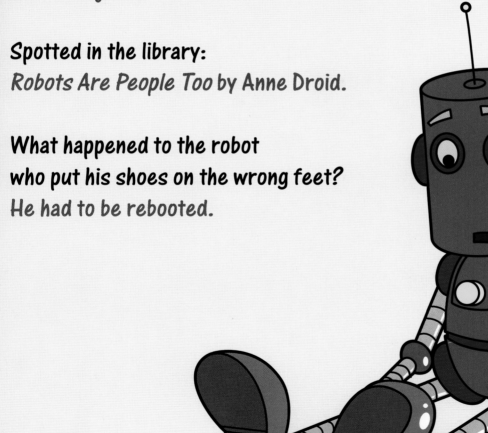

CRAZY COMPUTERS

What's orange and points North?
A magnetic carrot.

First robot: Are you enjoying that book about magnetism?
Second robot: Yes, I can't put it down!

Why was the thirsty astronaut hanging out near the computer keyboard?
He was looking for the space bar.

Did you hear about the couple who adopted a calculator?
It made a great addition to the family.

Why did the Apple Mac programmer live in the dark?
Because he refused to use Windows.

CRAZY COMPUTERS

Why did the boy bring a surfboard to school? The teacher said they were going to be surfing the Internet.

Why was the computer such a terrific golfer? It had a hard drive.

How do lumberjacks get on the Internet? They log on.

What do you call a man with a cable coming out of his ear? Mike!

What do you buy for someone who already has all the latest gadgets? A burglar alarm.

Why did the robot get angry? Someone kept pushing his buttons!

What do you get if you cross a large computer and a hamburger? A Big Mac!

Why do robots never feel queasy? They have cast iron stomachs.

Why did the pupil fall asleep in computer class? He was feeling key-bored.

What do you give a robot who feels like a light snack? Some 60 watt bulbs!

CRAZY COMPUTERS

What's the difference between computer hardware and software?
Hardware is the stuff that you can kick when it doesn't work.

What goes in one year and out the other?
A time machine!

Teacher: Give me an example of cutting edge technology.
Pupil: A pair of scissors?

My computer is powered by clockwork.
Really?
No, I was just winding you up.

What is a robot's favorite music?
Heavy metal!

CRAZY COMPUTERS

How can you tell if a robot is happy to see you?
Because his eyes light up.

What do you get from robot sheep?
Steel wool.

Why did the computer programmer give up his job?
He lost his drive.

Why was the electrified robot so badly behaved?
It didn't know how to conduct itself.

Did you hear about the robot dog?
His megabark was worse than his megabyte.

CRAZY COMPUTERS

What do you call a robot who turns into a tractor?
A trans-farmer!

Where do cool
mice live?
In mouse pads.

Did you know that
my computer can do
the gardening?
Can it really?
Yes, it's made
with cutting
hedge technology.

What is a baby
computer's first word?
Data.

Did you hear about the two TVs who got married?
Their reception was excellent.

CRAZY COMPUTERS

Why did the boy and girl robots call things off after their first date?
There was no spark.

Why did the robot kiss his girlfriend?
He just couldn't resistor.

How did the inventor of the jetpack feel?
He was on cloud nine!

Why did the storekeeper refuse to serve italic fonts?
He didn't like their type.

Where did the tightrope walker meet his girlfriend?
Online.

CRAZY COMPUTERS

How do snowmen get online?
They use the Winternet.

How does a tiny robot say goodbye?
With a micro-wave.

Brad: Have you seen my high-tech watch belt?
Suzie: It sounds like a waist of time.

Which way did the outlaw
go after he stole
the computer?
He went data way.

What do
astronauts
eat out of?
Satellite
dishes.

CRAZY COMPUTERS

What do you call a flying printer?
An inkjet.

Which city has no people?
Electricity.

Why should you not be upset if a computer beats you
at chess?
You can still beat it at table tennis.

Spotted in the library:
How to Build a Shrink Ray
by Minnie Mize.

Why did the witch buy
a computer?
She needed a spell-checker!

CRAZY COMPUTERS

Why don't elephants
use computers?
Because they are
scared of the mouse!

Which superhero will
get the creases out of
your pants?
Iron Man.

Why didn't the cheap
laptop work?
Because the battery
was given free
of charge.

How did the inventor of the space rocket feel?
Over the moon!

What flies through the air and tastes great with
peanut butter?
A jelly-copter.

CRAZY COMPUTERS

What kind of car does a robot drive?
A volts-wagon.

Mom robot: Stop being so antisocial and come down and meet our guests.
Son robot: I'm not antisocial—I'm just not user-friendly.

Why was the supercharged android so popular at parties?
He was a real live wire.

Doctor, I keep thinking I'm a computer.
Come into the hospital, then.
I can't, my power cable doesn't stretch that far.

Why couldn't the prisoner make a phone call?
His cell didn't have enough bars.

CRAZY COMPUTERS

Why did the strict mother put a sheet over the computer screen?
Because she didn't want her kids to pick up bad language from the cursor.

How do turtles stay in touch?
They use shell-ular phones.

Why did the computer throw its lunch in the garbage?
It looked like spam.

Why did the car blush?
It saw the traffic light changing.

What was the inscription on the robot grave?
"Rust in Pieces."

CRAZY COMPUTERS

How many ears does a robot have?
Three: a left ear, a right ear, and just in case they go wrong, an engine-ear.

What was wrong with the robot shepherd?
He didn't have enough RAM.

What do you call a man with a car on his head?
Jack!

How do you fix a robotic gorilla?
With a monkey wrench.

Why did the inventor stuff herbs in the disk drive of his computer?
He was trying to build a thyme machine.

CRAZY COMPUTERS

Why couldn't the computer take its hat off?
Because the caps lock was on.

Spotted in the library:
How to Fix Just About Anything by Andy Mann.

Teacher: Look at the state of the classroom computer. I want that screen cleaned so well I can see my own face in it!
Pupil: But then it will crack!

What do you call a short band leader?
A semi-conductor.

Why did the computer catch a cold?
Someone kept leaving its Windows open.

CRAZY COMPUTERS

Why did the robot swimmer have to practice so much?
Because he kept getting rusty.

Did you hear about the coffee-drinking robot?
Boy, was he ever wired!

Why did the steel robot have so many friends?
He had a magnetic personality.

Can you spell "user-friendly computer" in just four letters?
E, Z, P, C!

Where do cars go swimming?
In a carpool.

CRAZY COMPUTERS

Why shouldn't you trust someone who always types in upper case?
There is something very shifty about them.

Why did the P.C. keep sneezing?
It had a computer virus.

What was wrong with the environmentally friendly flashlight?
It relied on solar power.

Did you hear about the cyborg's expensive new limbs?
They cost him an arm and a leg!

Why do robots make great stuntmen?
Because they have nerves of steel.

CRAZY COMPUTERS

What do you call a man who never leaves his car?
Otto!

What do you call a robot standing in the rain?
Rusty!

What invention is sillier than glow-in-the-dark sunglasses
for midnight sunbathing?
Underwater umbrellas for scuba divers!

Why did the silly girl put her letters in the microwave?
She wanted to use Hotmail.

Why did they have
to call off the
computer race?
The competitors
kept crashing.

CRAZY COMPUTERS

Who won the Oscar for best android actor?
Robot Downey, Jr.

How did the scientist invent insect repellent?
He started from scratch.

There's never anything on TV, is there?
I don't know about that—there's a vase on top of ours.

Have you been on the optician's website?
It's a site for sore eyes.

Why did the computer programmer give up his life of crime?
He couldn't hack it any more.

What do you call a nervous robot?
A shy-borg.

How do lazy spiders decorate their homes?
They hire web designers.

Do you think scientists will ever invent flying desserts?
No, that's pie in the sky.

What happened when the bossy android charged for too long?
It went on a power trip!

How did the lazy office worker get his daily exercise?
He turned on his computer and clicked on "run."

CRAZY COMPUTERS

Teacher: Why have you stopped typing?
Pupil: It was making me feel keyed up.

Did you hear about the computer programmer whose illegal activities made him sick?
He gave himself a hacking cough.

Did you have any success with Internet dating?
Yes, it was love at first site.

Why didn't two computers get along?
They got their wires crossed.

What do you call an android with oars?
A row-bot.

CRAZY COMPUTERS

How did the computer get out of prison?
It used its "escape" key.

What is a sheep's favorite Internet site?
Ewe tube.

Why did the little robot start to cry?
He was missing his motherboard.

Do you think teleportation will ever be possible?
That's neither here nor there.

How do you catch a computer thief?
With a mousetrap.

CRAZY COMPUTERS

Did you hear
about the
unhappy android?
It had a chip on its shoulder!

Why did the computer
programmer call
pest control?
His software was
full of bugs!

Teacher: Can you
think of a password with
eight characters?
Pupil: How about "Snow White
and the Seven Dwarves?"

What sort of net do you use to catch robot fish?
A mag-net.

What do you call a robot pig?
A sty-borg.

What did one calculator say to the other calculator?
You can count on me.

What do robot office workers eat?
A staple diet.

Why did the girl mouse decide not to ask the boy mouse out on a second date?
They just didn't click.

Computer repair man: What's wrong with this laptop, sir?
Customer: Thespacebarseemstobestuck.

Have you heard about the new online service for short-sighted people?
It's called the Squinternet.

CRAZY COMPUTERS

Spotted in the library:
The Easy Way to Fly by Otto Pilot.

Why did the computer go crazy?
It had a screw loose.

How do you stop batteries from running out?
Hide their sneakers.

What do you call a robot that always takes the longest route?
R2 Detour.

Did you hear about the little robot
who looked just like his dad?
He was a microchip off the old block.

Glossary

byte (BYT) a measure of
electronic information used
by computer programmers

cyborg (SY-borg) a person with
robotic parts, or a robot with
human parts

hardware (HARD-wayr) tools
and machines

microchip (MY-kroh-chip) a small,
flat rectangle made of a hard
material, which can store
electronic information

megabyte (MEH-guh-byt) a measure
of electronic information equal
to about one million bytes

software (SOFT-wayr) computer
programs

Further Reading

Goldsmith, Mike, and Tom Jackson.
Computer. New York: DK
Publishing, 2011.

Gifford, Clive. *Robots.* New York:
Atheneum Books, 2008.

Howard, Megan. *Robots: The Joke
Book.* New York: Harper
Festival, 2005.

Index

Websites

For Web resources related to
the subject of this book, go to:
www.windmillbooks.com/weblinks
and select this book's title.